THE ART OF

SELLING

IT IS THE ART OF SHARING...

BECAUSE WE ALL SELL SOMETHING

FRANCISCO DI EMMANUEL

BUSINESS COACH, ARTIST AND FRIEND

FRANCISCO DI EMMANUEL

THE ART OF SELLING

HOW TO SELL?

FIRST EDITION 2020

©2020 AUTHOR'S RIGHTS RESERVED

Thanks:

TO GOD...

To my beautiful GOD who has never abandoned me on my way, and who continues to teach me in his own way every day.

TO MY MOTHER...

To my MOTHER who did not abandon me in that hospital, but she fought every day with all her love so that I could geta head and be a good man.

TO MY FATHER...

That taught me how to fly from the nest, with my wings renewed. And it taught me the secret of living well from my talent.

TO MY THREE POST MOMS...

GRANDMA FRANCIS, FRANCIS RINCÓN AND SUSI RINCÓN

That they took care of me protected and taught like another mom.

TO GLORIELITA RAZ GUZMAN...

Big Godmother... (Also post mom)

That helped me many times to heal my emotional wounds and woke me up for writing.

TO MY BROTHERS:

IVÁN, PACO, CARLITOS Y HILL…

But above all to: <u>**IVÁN RINCÓN**</u> who was the best of the older brothers and who took care of me, guided and supported me, as a good older brother really should be.

THANKS:

I want to thank my students as a writer and artist in Sales, that without their requests, this material would not have been possible, I thank all my teachers who taught me very well the art of selling but above all the art of bringing peace and joy to others through sales.

Thanks to all the sales friends who collaborated with their anecdotes of life and their experience. Thank God that he accompanies me throughout my journey and never abandons me.

Thanks to my parents who instilled in me never to stay on one path but to continue investigating how we can improve.

And thanks to you that today you are enjoying this beautiful book. I hope it will be of great help to you and share your talent with others.

Congratulations
Your personal Sales Coach:

FRANCISCO DI EMMANUEL

1# BELIEVE IN YOURSELF

Have confidence in yourself, the most powerful weapon that a seller has within your reach, is the confidence you place in yourself and the confidence you can create in the people who are listening to you.

Without trust we are nothing. With confidence we are everything, and for that you have to dress, talk and feel like a winner, because you are, you have in your hands the possibility of improving life for you and your customers.

Dressing well improves your self-esteem, but dressing well according to what you sell improves your sales...

You are a sales artist, you must go out into the world with your best smile and your best wardrobe, those clothes that represent what you sell, your gala suit, your tuxedo, your hanger uniform, your best dress, shined shoes, hairstyle of winner and winner.

Because the world before hearing what you have for them, they will first see you from top to bottom, and they will see you as a winner and they will want to know about you and what you are selling. And they will be eager to know what you have to offer.

Jump to sell and devour the world to bites.

HOW THEY SEE YOU TREAT YOU

YOUR IMAGE ALSO SELLS

Your image is your way of dressing, as lights, if you are well groomed or not, if you dress formally or not, what your clothes say about you and your body language (how you stand, how you walk, etc.).

Your Image is your first impression before the client, the first key to be able to sell big.

Your image sells and sells very well. What's more, before you approach people to try to make a sale, they already saw you from top to bottom, analyzed you, and in a matter of seconds, they formed an idea of you. You didn't have to say anything yet, but they already judged you for better or for worse, and they kept you in their minds in the good or bad zone of their mind that depends on you.

Remember that you are your product and your image is the most important thing to be able to open the dialogue towards a sale. Your image builds trust and if you look your best, people will allow you to get closer to interacting with them. Otherwise prepare yourself for endless rejections: No thanks, I have no change or you are not what I am looking for thanks.

I have an engineer friend who is a great programmer but he is always unemployed or he doesn't work very long, he is a great computer engineer, but he just doesn't like to wear formal clothes. His favorite clothes for him are his torn black sneakers, his denim pants and his white t-shirts, with that he feels super comfortable and is fine, it is important to feel comfortable while you work, but it does not cover at all the standards of a company of High Prestige.

We know that the image of a company is not only its product, but also its employees. Imagine that you visited the company and I will introduce you to the Systems Engineer dressed like this. What would be your first impression of him? Would you believe me he's an engineer dressed like this? Of course not, right?

The same goes for your way of dressing; it represents not only who you are but what you sell.

Imagine that you want to get the best job in the world. Be the Chief or Director of that luxury company and earn the millions that the Chief earns; and you show up for your pants and shirt interview Mmm... ... what do you think, do you think they would give you the job?

Right?

This book was created so that you would be financially free and that you would not spend your whole life receiving a small salary as an employee. But you will earn more, much more, thanks to your skills and attitudes.

And it is that although you do not believe it:

> **YOUR IMAGE SELLS AND SELLS VERY WELL.**

For example, I always do my job dressed in a suit and tie and it is not only because it makes me feel comfortable, but it gives me confidence when it comes to selling and confidence is power.

It is as if the client has a special power to feel your vibe, and if you feel good about yourself (looking great and clean), your client will perceive it and will be more attracted to what you sell.

I can swear to you that this advice will do.

It helps me a lot, especially when negotiating a price or closing a deal. It seems like a lie but it is not, the mere fact of wearing a tie or not, makes my client not see me the same.

When I don't wear a tie I look informal and most of the cases have rejected me when offering my product. It seems like magic, I'm just going to put on my tie or bowtie and customers start to fall wanting to hire my services. It's an internal matter; call it that, but dressing well works. It also helps me differentiate myself from the competition; my service is of the highest quality. And my clothing reflects what I do.

As my old teacher said:

> NOT TO SMELL YOUR NEED TO SMELL YOUR PRESTIGE ...

It is like the boy who wants to conquer the girl and the first thing that the young lady must pay attention to is the boy's footwear.

If, when he goes on a date with her, he brings the shoes on… he means that he is a clean boy and attentive to details, but if he brings all the careless shoes, that girl is sure to suffer with him.

So it is very important that you learn to sell and your clothes sell.

Now, that's what I did, but if you dedicate yourself to selling bread, for example, dress as a baker that gives confidence and attracts many more customers.

I know the best story in the world, a man who was drowning in debt but took advantage of his new way of dressing...

LEARN TO ENTERPRISE

This is the true story of a man who was drowning in debt.

> **"ENTERPRISE OR DIE"**

LEARN TO ENTERPRISE

This is the true story of a man who was drowning in debt.

"ENTERPRISE OR DIE"

Every day he increased the debt on his cards and was about to lose his house due to the increase in interest on his debt. The banks kept calling him at home and insisting that he would pay them.

He worked as an employee in a company, but his salary was not enough to cover all his needs.

One desperate day, he had to decide or invest what little money he had left to do something that would make him more money or spend the few coins he had and only eat three more days.

The decision was easy: invest your money to survive.

So a great idea occurred to him: 6 days a week he went to work around 9 in the morning to his formal job, and on that same street a huge number of people passed who were also going to their jobs.

These people also needed to eat, so he decided that the next day, with the little money he had left, he would make some bread with ham and cheese to sell. And sell them as breakfast to people who were going to work.

This meant that he had to get up in the morning to bake the breads, prepare the food and arrive much earlier on the street where the people were walking; to try to sell everything from 8 to 9 in the morning before his usual work begins.

I needed to get attention. So he got some cloth that he had lying around, and made a Red Apron and a huge Hat like a baker or chef (HIS CLOTHING SOLD) and went out to sell, now yes, it was very striking and seeing his hat From chef, people thought his breads were delicious.

These looked very good and that day he sold all his merchandise.

That day with what little he had he had made 12 loaves, for the next day with what he won he proposed to make 10 more loaves. Every day he would increase the number of loaves from 10 to 10 to see how many he could sell, so he grew. One day even new people came to ask him for a job, because of how much he sold. So he started hiring more people and selling and selling.

Soon, not only did he pay off all his debts, but he employed more people like him than needed, built a society, and started his own business. You see how in this story the clothing made it attract more attention and its sales will rise to the top.

YOUR CLOTHING SELLS

YOUR TALENT MAY BE, YOU'RE BEST ENTREPRENEURSHIP…

This story happened to someone close to me, a friend from my job named Victor who also drowned in debt loved to be asking and borrowing from others and never paid them, how? If he never had money, and what he earned from his salary he already owed.

One day, my other friend Luis warned me that I would never lend Victor a dollar, because I would never see that dollar again.

The least expected day arrived, where Victor asked the wrong person for money.

It turns out that it occurred to Victor to borrow from Esmeralda the Secretary and Victor did not know but Esmeralda was the boss's spoiled girlfriend.

Imagine that one day Esmeralda arrived very angry, because she had loaned money to Victor two months ago, and he does not deign to pay him. And that if in the next fortnight he did not pay Esmeralda's wife, she was going to notify her boyfriend (The Head of our company) to put him on the street, that is, to fire him.

As we appreciated our friend despite his defect, we went and told him that he will already pay Esmeralda, because if he did not pay off his debt in 15 days, he would notify the Chief and it is certain that if they ran it.

Although Victor's work was related to something administrative, right there in the company there were several workshops for the beneficiaries who came to that place, such as painting, drawing, music, among others.

Victor liked to dance a lot in his spare time and electronic music was his passion.

So it occurred to him to open his new workshop, right there in the company in the afternoons, it was called "Cardio Dance" and it was about cardiovascular exercises with electronic music and a little dance.

My friend was a success from the beginning, he started charging $ 5 pesos per person, in the first week he had 30 ladies, but by the second week the word spread and he already had 70 ladies in a single hour of class.

My friend Victor not only quickly paid Esmeralda for the secretary, but he earned it, because in order to keep her happy and on his side, he let her take his free Cardio Dance classes.

My friend started doing very well, with his first earnings and he sent himself to make some Instructor t-shirts... Remember:

> "DRESS ACCORDING TO WHAT YOU DO SELL..."

He paid for a few instructor classes, and what he was learning he was teaching in his own private classes. It soon became so popular that after filling the maximum capacity of 70 people in the ballroom, it had to open a second shift also full of 70 other people:

Ladies and gentlemen and young people all wanted to be in your classes.

I even apply the strategy of not allowing access to those who were not enrolled in the list, and you also had to take care of your place, because if they filled up earlier, with the 70 people that was the maximum capacity of the place, you had to stand in line and wait your turn until the second class.

It was incredible to see how people lined up to wait their turn for the class that followed, many women did not care if it rained or it was cold, they just took care of their place.

People really paid their full week, so they could have the privilege of being in that class.

I think that the success of everything was that the cost of the classes was not very high, and people sweated literally like soup.

In a few weeks I believe out of nowhere, a profitable business, more or less you have accounts, if you already had two shifts of 70 people, that is to say 140 people in your two classes for $ 5 pesos that you charged, they are 140 people x $ 5 pesos = a $ 700 daily pesos, for 5 days a week are $ 3,500 pesos working only two hours, from Monday to Friday and resting on weekends.

That without adding the sale of the shirts and records, which he sold at the end of his class.

That is to say that at the end of the month, he had many sources of income: One as an Instructor of his Workshop, two, in the sale of sportswear, three, the electronic music records specialized for doing Fitness, and four, his basic salary for his managerial job at the company in the morning.

It was a Super Profitable business, imagine every Saturday he went to his fitness trainer classes, and what he knew he applied all the following week with his students, the music was given to him in the same school, so he did not spend time doing it.

He was also always super honest with his students, he said that he was not an expert, and that he was still going to classes to learn, how to be a great coach, and that he only applied what they taught him at school.

This was inadvertently a great marketing hit and promotion for his workshop, because many people gladly paid for his class to support the good work of the teacher.

It was like a win - win:

> "I SUPPORT YOU AND YOU SUPPORT ME (WIN WIN)"

THE UNIFORM

The uniform, let's call it that, or the clothes you wear to represent what you do, will always help you sell more, and give people even more confidence to buy from you.

My musician friends for example, always wear suits and bow ties, they look super elegant, and on the back of their jackets they embroidered the name of the band they represent.

Imagine a Mariachi; you agree that it would not be a complete Mariachi without the corresponding charro suit and hat.

I think I cannot imagine and I feel that it would not be to my liking if the Mariachi came to my house, with all my guests, ready for the music and that the Mariachi was dressed in denim.

See what I say they could play and sing very well but without the charro suit, I feel deep down in my heart, like something is missing, don't you think?

When I was a child I loved going to a cinema especially...

A huge cinema that turned it into a Castle on the Outside! Full of characters and images from your favorite children's movies. It was as if we were in the square of the stars but for children, it was beautiful.

There were even stars on the floor, with the names of the characters, you know that Hollywood type and you could touch them and stand there.

I loved going to that cinema, plus there was a huge toy store next to it.

Whenever we arrived, my family and I went into the toy store first, bought an ice cream and went straight to the cinema.

Everyone who worked there wore a beanie and a shirt with the "Magic Cinema" logo. Even when there were premieres, some employees dressed like the characters in the movie.

PURE MARKETING:

> The clothes, the logos, the stars and the form that the cinema has as a castle are pure marketing to attract customers, especially children, and why not? Also to adults and their inner child.
>
> ALL THIS SELLS.

A SMILE OPENS THE GATES OF THE WORLD

That's true after dressing, which will make a person like you more; it's a good smile and a reliable greeting.

It is very likely that from the beginning people will not shake your hand, but with a good smile and a cheerful and cordial greeting, you can open the dialogue to achieve the sale.

Service and friendliness come first, you don't know how many sellers I see, who know this but don't apply it; First they arrive with the client, they greet very kindly, smiling and they even tell him a joke, and the client laughs, they like him, but in the end they don't close the sale, they get angry, they talk and they leave very upset saying things under their breath As if the client was not listening.

This is very bad, because you leave a bad impression of falsehood to the customer. This then, then thinks: - that seller was not sincere, he was just being nice for me to buy from him, but since I didn't want to, he left very angry, as if buying from him even if I didn't want to, was forced.

- And you will have lost a client who perhaps at that time did not need your product, but you do not know if later on, and you will have chased him away with your bad ways. Remember:

"WE ALL NEED EVERYONE"

If you act like this, although people may not believe it if they remember you, even if you don't remember them. You as a seller see and talk to millions of people a day, but what a customer remembers most about you, is a bad experience, bad service or a bad sale. Never get mad, don't even speak under your breath if you don't make the sale.

This is a big mistake, you don't know how many times people have said no to me, and a few moments later they say yes.

It has happened to me, that even some clients until the fifth time I have visited them say yes, four times in a row they told me no, and until the 5th time they are already ready to say yes, to buy and buy my service.

> "PEOPLE DON'T KNOW
>
> WHAT DOES A PRODUCT NEED?
>
> UNTIL A NEED IS GENERATED..."

You have to find the right moment where the customer feels comfortable to buy from you. Never lose faith. You have done your job well and the client will return to you.

For every satisfied customer there are at least 3 new customers to whom this customer will recommend...

But think that for every bad sale you make, there are at least 10 new clients with whom this same client can mention you... but with a bad recommendation to others... It is easier for the client to keep a bad recommendation in his mind.

In other words, for every satisfied customer there are 3 possible new sales.

And for every dissatisfied customer there are 10 sales that may not be achieved, just because of a bad attitude or a bad recommendation by that same customer.

Once I felt so beautiful, because a family came who liked my music very much.

But they told me that on that occasion they would not hire me, because their grandfather was very sick in the hospital, and he is the one who likes live music.

I told them that they would not worry, that if they liked we could make a video call with grandpa, and I would sing to him live. That's how we did it, they asked me for a bolero long ago but very beautiful of those who sang in the serenades in the films of the Mexican gold cinema.

Grandpa looked very happy on the phone.

They told me how much did they owe me $$$? And I told them that at the moment it was nothing, that when Grandpa recovered, they would bring him to eat at the restaurant and yes, they would ask me for many more songs (You have to sow love to reap love).

To my surprise two weeks later the whole family returned, including the grandfather and in gratitude, the family hired me all afternoon.

That was a very pleasant experience, although at work there are also experiences that are not to my liking but make you grow as a person and never repeat them, like the following anecdote:

I remember perfectly how working with the one who was my boss, an elderly man, very curmudgeons by the way, they had asked us for three songs for $ 200 pesos, at the end of those three songs the client was so happy, that she said please, As his brothers were at the party that day, we gave him one more song. At that moment I told my boss what the lady told me, that if we gave him "La Bamba" because that song liked his brothers and the lady.

To which my boss replied very angry and with a strong voice:

- are you crazy? I do not give my work to anyone. If you want to sing it, but not me. - I died of grief because my boss spoke very loudly and the client heard everything. She spoke to me and said: - Look, I will hire you again for being nice and attentive, but I will hire that man (that is to say, my boss) in life. As you see a bad impression it is very difficult to solve. It took us over 1 year for that lady to hire us again.

Coincidence? I do not think so.

The recommendations that people make to you on your channel or virtual page that is different and is good, there people anonymously and online can make positive or negative comments about whether or not they liked your product, if they delivered it on time Or if the seller was kind to the buyer, from all those comments take note and improve your sale or your product.

Like the following comment, example:

I loved going on vacation to the best beach in Mexico. Lots of glamour.

A paradise, great service, great banquets, great food, excellent beaches and tourist attractions. Do you know what I left owed in some places...? With a smile and with thanks come back soon.

Everything was excellent, but those simple magic words improve everything. As they say courteous does not take away the brave and a good smile will make you fall in love forever. Long live my Mexico its beautiful beaches and its people. (Anonymous)

GIVE THEM A TEST OF YOUR TALENT

I love this part of the job; this is where you discover who is and who not your potential client is.

I love it because when I give them a test of my talent I can see how people react, in my case I am a musician and my test of talent is to sing a song outdoors before going to the tables to offer my work.

I do it for two things, one to get the attention of the client and know that there is quality in what I sell, and two to discover who can be my best prospects to be my clients. That is to say, to whom I have more possibilities to sell.

It is like throwing a small hook, so that whoever catches it, buys me.

It is a lot of fun, because when singing, at the same time I am analyzing people: as you saw, what kind of music is it that you might like...

As you know I sing from many genres and not all people like the same thing.

Some even hide, like they shrink when I turn to see them. If I see that they cover their ears or look for their cell phone, as if to hide that they don't listen to me, those clients will almost certainly not hire me.

But I also invite them to hire me later, to be my next clients.

Normally if they say no, I tell them not to worry, see you at dessert, or to please recommend us, that there in the restaurant we have live music and a family member may be interested.

Some birthday, some baptism etc.

It has happened to me that many of these clients but hire me; bring me a friend and family member who do like my product which is music.

There are even some clients who when I take their eyes off them, I feel that they take confidence and turn to me, they are looking at me, that means that if they like my work.

Some even sing with me, those are the most potential clients that I find.

For example, once a boy came in with a girl, I offered him my songs and he said no, that at that time he had no money.

He told me that he only went to the restaurant to listen to me sing, live, for which I insisted, so to hire me I said, you can hire me from a song.

He said no, but then he would come back with lots of money and hire me.

He fulfilled it, sometime later he returned, after 6 months he returned to the restaurant with a super pretty girl, who told me that she was his girlfriend. I contract 5 hours straight, right there in the restaurant.

I do not know if they paid him very well or asked for his loan to the bank, but he sang with me happily and loudly the mariachi music and threw $ 500 pesos bills all over the table. I was happy and I was too, because that day he paid me very well for my work.

At the end he said to me: - do you remember that I told you that one day I would come with my girlfriend and sing with you all afternoon? Well that day is today!

- As you can never see and despise any client, no matter how they look or how old they are. If they do not hire you, just tell them good it will be for the next thanks.

Sometimes, in addition to being a salesman and a musician, I have had to work as a psychologist or as a listener.

There was a client who was coming very sad, he asked me to sit at his table, and he was going to pay me whatever but please listen to him. I said yes.

Being at his table he told me that he felt very sad because he always went to that restaurant, he listened to me sing and he never hired me and then... zaz! Started crying. Poor really was very bad and I wanted to help him, I asked him what was wrong with him? And he told me that he owned a very important company and that he felt very sad because his fiscal year had not done very well in his sales and his company was going bankrupt.

In addition, the next day he had to fire more than 200 people from his job (the people who worked for him).

He was very sad, inconsolable, and already a little taken. He wanted to drown his sorrows in alcohol and songs, but he needed someone to listen to him:

So I heard it... (Not everything is money...)

He told me how he suffered, because he knew that he had to fire them all very soon.

I just listened to him, and I said, can I give you some advice if you allow me? He said yes. I understand that you need to fire all those people for your company to survive, I said, but your employees are the heart and engine of your company. If it is inevitable that you have to fire them, please ask to speak to them before doing so. They deserve to know the reason for their layoffs and to prepare; they and their families will have to look for another job. My client was relieved and promised he would do the talking.

Four months later I saw him again... he went to celebrate at my restaurant where I work. He told me that the next day he spoke to me. He held an emergency meeting and asked that all employees be present.

He explained that due to lack of resources, the company had to close and liquidate all its employees, that it was very sorry to fire them but could no longer pay them more than the coming fortnight and no more. Well, there were no resources to get the product and pay the workers.

The employees did not want to leave their jobs, they loved working for that company, and many had been working there for years. So after talking with each other they reached a mutual agreement. They would work that month even without charging their last fortnight of the month, if possible up to overtime, but they will be able to get the entire product that the company needed to survive.

So they were, the company came out ahead thanks to the love and effort of all its workers. They managed to get the product out on time and my client, the owner of the company, was able to pay all his employees what he owed them. He in gratitude gift pantries to his most outstanding employees the following Christmas.

Do not be afraid to show your talent, many who are from my competition only play a little, half a song and they already go on to offer songs, but that is not right, it is like tasting a dessert and after they take it from you, the emotion is lost.

I prefer to play a complete song, surprise my client and now yes, to offer my product, go to the safe. I call it collecting what you sowed.

> "YOU WILL ALWAYS COLLECT WHAT YOU SOWED"

Offering a little of your talent or product is very good and this is known by Chinese sales experts. You see that when you are in a shopping plaza and you go to see what there is to eat, always in Chinese food, they give you a taste of their sweet and sour chicken, a ball of food on a small stick.

This is a great marketing trick, you are already there, you tried their food and there is a 95% that you buy from them and there are no others for the commitment that you accepted their food.

Also if by it, you were already hungry, that little ball of chicken whet your appetite and your brain says - yes, if you no longer look to eat, eat!

- It is a great trick to sell; all fast food companies have one.

But we will talk about that later.

PEOPLE ARE PREPARED TO SAY NO

People are predisposed to tell you no, don't worry and persevere.

"LEARN TO SELL"

Something that marked me forever is "LEARNING TO SELL" really, no matter what you do, you can be super professional in what you do, with many studies. But if you don't know how to sell, you literally don't do anything, or you'll always have to be someone else's employee.

Also, something they never teach you in school is learning to sell.

And although you may not believe it all, absolutely WE ALL SELL SOMETHING, maybe it is a service, a product, a query etc. We all exchange time for money. Some more than 8 hours in a row in a job that they do not like, for a salary that is barely enough to live on. That is indeed slavery!

If that is your case friend, you need to learn to sell and this is the book to achieve it.

The first thing DOES NOT BE AFRAID OF THE FAMOUS NO...

It really is horrible, for me it was very easy to stand on stage and sing, as a song should. But get off the stage and offer my work from table to table. It was terrible.

I was very scared.

"WE ALL SELL SOMETHING"

I remember that my Head of Musicians was a curmudgeon, besides that he exploited me because he always kept my tips and 70% of my earnings. I got the clients and he kept everything. So I had to learn how to sell.

I remember that I went to the restaurant on a Monday; I went alone to sing and sell my songs. The first time it cost me a lot of work and grief. I did everything right, I sang the best song I knew, I was applauded, and I approached a client who looked cool to offer my product.

I introduced myself (Hi, I'm Fracisco Di Emmanuel and I'll be your singer-songwriter this afternoon...) I offered him my job, and he said yes.

To top it off, as always, they ask you for the song you least know. But since that was my first client, I said yes. I went to the internet on my Smartphone, to listen to the song that he asked me and I returned with the client.

He told me that that was his favorite song, that if he had it, if he hired me, but if it wasn't that, then a.

Well I sang it as I could; I was so worried about my performance that the truth came out terrible.

When I finished the song I was so nervous. That the client said to me: - the truth did not come out to you too, but… you did your best, you even looked it up on the internet.

So I will pay you. - He gave me a medium bill, I thanked him and with that same bill I ran away, but to my house of shame. Why? Yes of the 1,000 songs that I know, why exactly did you ask me for one that you didn't know? Why?

The truth is that it is an experience, and I honestly didn't have that song worked on. He was also the first client and with him that I wanted to make a sale, I was completely alone. It was not selling what made me feel ashamed, what made me sad and very afraid is the possible rejection, "no thanks, for the moment I think no, I have no change, after a while, on the way back, etc. etc. etc." Have you ever heard something like that? Raise your hand please if so, so I don't feel like I'm the only one… thanks.

Total thousands of excuses that people put to you to say no.

Some even told me I have no change or I bought you after a while, after a while I would ask them again and they would tell me now if after a while, when I came back after a while... they had already fled and they never bought me.

There are really people who don't know how to say no to you, and they bring you back and forth, hoping that they will buy you something.

Why do they do that? I think they see you as so nice that they don't know how to say no, they are sorry to tell you that they are not interested in your product at that time. But they don't want to hurt your feelings that are why they tell you the famous in a little while... And they bring you round and round...

Please don't do that.

Today when people say to me: - no thanks, I have no change...

-I tell them, don't worry, I'm already an entrepreneur... Here's my terminal!

> ## "IMPROVE YOURSELF"

My work changed a lot from being an Artist. I had to literally learn HOW TO SELL.

I read a lot of sales books, I went to conferences with the best sellers in the world, but what made me a great seller was the same practice of selling.

You will never achieve the succulent profits you deserve unless you lose your fear of selling

Selling is not bad, simply selling is the exchange of one good for another good or service.

I soon learned a lot about sales. I even worked on my SPEECH (My Sales Speech). When he saw a customer with a glass of wine, he would tell him. Good evening, Lord, the geniuses tell us ... The client answered -why? - Because they uncover a bottle and we appear as if by magic...

The client liked him, some even laughed at me, a funny comment that he had just said.

Did people trust you...? Now it is time to sell your product.

"WORK YOUR SPEECH"

Normally if you get to sell, as such sell, people are predisposed to say no, even before you tell them your speech people have already thought about how to reject your offer.

There are thousands of sellers in the world, so much so that people are even super predisposed to tell you no.

They smell your salesman smell.

Eye! I said there are thousands of sellers in the world...

> **"BUT NONE LIKE YOU…**
>
> **"So you have to make a difference"**

I know they need good sellers in this world.

My simplest and easiest sales have been when I don't try to sell. Or when I sell without selling, for example I look for what people might want; I analyze what their needs are. If I see a couple with a baby or a child. I do not come and I say: good afternoon look I have many songs for children, this is the music menu and I know this and I know the other, no.

Do you usually know what they are going to tell me? No thanks.

The secret instead, is that I see that they bring a baby, so the priority is the baby, I sell the baby. How do I do it?

Very easy, I don't say anything and I sing a nice song for children, that is, I sell the child without saying anything, I sing to the baby, normally the boy or girl likes the song and shakes his head up and down, or dances, or clap, or laugh, the child is happy. And if you have a detail with the children, normally the parents have a detail with you, which are summarized in money or profit.

Ok the song ends, the boy is happy, and now yes, I go to the table, normally the parents give me a ticket or hire me 3 songs or more. You see I made an unsold sale.

"SELL IT TO THE RIGHT PERSON"

This tool is to sell to the right person, like the child in the previous example, I learned it when I worked for a very large chain of cinemas, there the business is not the sale of tickets, since most of the profits are taken by the creators from movies and distributors.

The profit for movie theaters and movie theater staff is actually selling the popcorn, candy and soda they sell inside the movie theaters themselves.

When you get to buy from the candy store, you don't have to sell to the boyfriend, sell to the girl who comes with him. The latter will buy everything that the bride asks for, because the boy wants to get on well with the girl.

The same goes for children, when the parents come to buy, do not sell to the parents, and sell to the child. Dads will buy anything as long as their son or daughter is happy and calm to watch the movie.

"HAVE SOMETHING IN COMMON WITH THE CLIENT"

Many times I have made a big unsold sale. One day I came to offer my services to a table of a family of many members. Then, later, they told me no, I told them I don't want to be indiscreet but that they have nice uniforms for the children. What club are they from? To what they said: - we are not from any club, they are our church shirts, we serve God from childhood. - I was very sincere and I told them I also serve God (every job I do I dedicate to him, to my higher power) and every Sunday I sing in the church near my house.

I suppose they felt confident, I was honest with my words, not only for selling, in truth I also believe in a higher power and support for the community of my church. I think they felt great confidence in me and that we had something in common, because that same afternoon they hired me like twelve songs or more.

> **"ALWAYS BE AN HONEST AND SINCERE SELLER"**

I started my career in sales from a very young age, and one of my first formal sales jobs was "Furniture and White Goods Salesman". I really liked that job, I learned a lot of things from it, and I owe a lot of those things to my boss. Of floor, he was a man like 1.60 tall, very skinny but leathery and of an advanced age, that's why we said to him of affection the grandfather, he still had his black hair, with very few gray hairs, but we always suspected that he painted his hair .

I confess to you that when I first came to that company I applied for the job as a box seller, but if I have always looked younger than I am, when I came to apply for a job I was just 18 years old, so I still looked younger and the Human Resources Manager made me a challenge.

He told me that if he accepted the job in furniture and white goods and he saw that he had commitment and dedication in 6 months.

The same Resource Manager would find a way to move me to the cashier department.

I told him what - what should he do?

And he said to me: - Well, first you have to earn your place

-How? Answer is it to say that I don't have a secure job?

-Of course not, you have to earn it, all workers start like this, and you go to one of the best sales departments of this company.

So you will be a month of trial. If your boss gives me good recommendations from you, I will extend your contract to 3 more months and if you pass the trial period, then and only then will you have your place.

-And what will happen to the box department? I asked for:

-After you go through all that process and depending on how you have performed in a maximum of 6 months I can transfer you to boxes.

-All right, I accept, I answered and I shook his hand with a strong squeeze.

At first I did not think that it was necessary to have as much procedure to move to the department that I wanted, but now I think that what the Human Resources Manager did was the best, not only hiring a person like me who wanted to learn and work very hard, It also gave me the motivation to achieve all my goals together with the company, and a motivated person can achieve anything.

I learned a lot of things, but what helped me the most was learning to sell from person to person.

It is horrible when a customer goes to a shopping center, interested in a specific item and the floor vendor has not done his homework, that is, he does not know anything about the products he sees with him day by day.

It accommodates them, cleans them from dust, and offers them to the public and when you finally ask them for a technical detail, YOU KNOW NOTHING! He always tells you, let me see, and he looks for him and he looks for the box (that means that he has not studied his product) or he says wait for me a bit, I will speak to the manager of the department, and he goes and never comes back, because he is the one floor manager.

Has it happened to you? Well, in this company it was not like that, and it does have a lot to do with the worker, I was super motivated to learn everything about my department and my product because I wanted to earn that place. I think that's why Grandpa (my boss) liked me and taught me everything he knew. Just as you looked skinny and old, he loaded the highest refrigerators, he alone, he said that he was not force but skill when loading, and he was right.

Of course we always walked with a belt and our security team to load insurance inside the warehouse. And a separate shirt, always clean to go to the sales floor.

I liked it a lot because apart from selling mattresses, washing machines and refrigerators, the furniture came unarmed and we had to put it together to leave a sample.

This helped us a lot, because the people who were going to buy gave us good tips if we tied his mattress to the ceiling and even better if we put together a complete piece of furniture and sent it to him that way, armed at home. People paid well to save some time and work.

Many people came and asked especially for me, they even learned my name, and they did not let another seller attend them, and honesty is extremely important when it comes to selling. It happened to me that other sellers always tried to sell the most expensive product to the customer, when the customer was not really looking for that, or did not fit his budget.

Or many times they lied when it came to selling, adding additional applications to the product that they did not really have. That was really bad because the customer returned the product to the store when they discovered that their device was not actually doing what the seller was saying. That generated losses and a bad reputation because of other bad sellers. So rule number 1 when it comes to selling is to always be honest. There is no point lying for wanting to make a sale, you can fool people once, but they will never trust you again and therefore they will never buy anything from you again.

Trust is very important and I think that's why they approached me.

Whenever the promoters came, I would go to them to hear how they sold their product and the characteristics it had, in addition to the time they spent free, they would read the instructions for the devices for sale to learn how they were used, and to be able to explain well to the client its functions.

Most importantly, I always sold to the customer what their needs really asked of me.

For example, if they asked me for a 5-kilo washing machine with blades of water without blades, but the lady told me that her husband was a mechanic and wanted to use the washing machine to put his jeans there, that washing machine would not work for him. Then he offered her what she needed and explained why.

I said to him: look if you like, I can sell you this washing machine, but in reality it will not serve you for what you need, because it does not have blades and its capacity for clothing is very limited, it is for simple clothes, shirts or baby clothes.

"AWARD FOR HONESTY"

I offer you this one, which is worth a little more but has the capacity and the power that you occupy so that you can wash those heavy denim pants. Maybe that day I did not sell that small washing machine, but in 5 days the same lady returned to me and asked me for the largest washing machine she had.

If you summarize it in earnings by being honest, I earned more, because I kept a customer happy and in the end the lady took the biggest washing machine, so the commission was bigger for me. Once again it was a great win - win

So it is very important that you always be honest with your client.

"SINCERITY AWARD"

IT'S NOT WHAT YOU SAY BUT HOW YOU SAY IT

As you saw in the last chapter, people are predisposed to say no, they are already self-programmed like this, it is like a defense mechanism, if they want it, they will do everything to get it, but if they do not want it.

It is your job to make them change their minds.

For that it is good that you practice a good speech, especially something nice and that you like. Something that allows you to get closer to the client without leaving it terrified.

Once a very nice young man came to me, however as I am a salesman with an expert eye, before he approached me, I already knew that something wanted to sell me. But out of professional curiosity I let him speak.

It could be seen that he had taken a sales course or someone was teaching him to sell because his speech was traced to others that I have already heard. However at first glance, the boy was friendly and attentive, good point for him, his clothing was youthful but clean and well groomed.

Everything very well except the speech ... It started like this: - Excuse me, can I ask you a favor? - That made me stop, to pay attention to you, until then very well, - I see that you are a very attractive person, I think you are very handsome, Would you like to go out with me?

- No thanks, I said, and he answered me - No, it's not true. Look, I'm a young entrepreneur who is selling these popsicles to help himself a little in this economy. - He took out some super ugly and expensive popsicles. And how much are they worth, I asked him?

- A $ 20 pesos 3 pieces for $ 50. - I ended up saying no thanks is that I hardly go to the work (maybe I would have bought him a popsicle to help him, but in reality he didn't want his popsicles at first sight they were sad they looked horrible)

Better I decided to help him, they say don't give him the fish, teach him how to fish, and I teach him how to fish a very big fish, that would feed him all his life, "Knowing how to sell" I came back with the boy and I said, "Excuse me, can I give you some advice?" Look I had to learn the art of selling from a very young age and the truth is that you are a very nice boy and you can see that you make an effort to learn, you remind me a little of me in my beginnings, that's why I want to tell you this: Your clothing is very good, you are a very charismatic boy, the problem is your speech...

You must analyze the person you are going to sell to before interacting with them. Well let's see, when you told me hey excuse me I can ask you a favor, you got my full attention, people like to help another as a matter of course, that was very good.

However you lost me when you flattered me the wrong way. You said hey you are very handsome; would you like to go out with me?

You lost me there because your intention was to make a joke, but I felt a bit harassed, in addition to not knowing you and it is rare that someone on the street asks you to go out with you without even knowing you.

It could be seen that he had taken a sales course or someone was teaching him to sell because his speech was traced to others that I have already heard. However at first glance, the boy was friendly and attentive, good point for him, his clothing was youthful but clean and well groomed. Everything very well except the speech...

It started like this: - Excuse me, can I ask you a favor? - That made me stop, to pay attention to you, until then very well, - I see that you are a very attractive person, I think you are very handsome, Would you like to go out with me?

- No thanks, I said, and he answered me –

No, it's not true. Look, I'm a young entrepreneur who is selling these popsicles to help himself a little in this economy. - He took out some super ugly and expensive popsicles.

And how much are they worth, I asked him? - A $ 20 pesos 3 pieces for $ 50.

- I ended up saying no thanks is that I hardly go to the chamber (maybe I would have bought him a popsicle to help him, but in reality he didn't want his popsicles at first sight they were sad they looked horrible) Better I decided to help him, they say don't give him the fish , teach him how to fish, and I teach him how to fish a very big fish, that would feed him all his life, "Knowing how to sell" I came back with the boy and I said,

"Excuse me, can I give you some advice?" Look I had to learn the art of selling from a very young age and the truth is that you are a very nice boy and you can see that you make an effort to learn, you remind me a little of me in my beginnings, that's why I want to tell you this: Your clothing is very good, you are a very charismatic boy, the problem is your speech…

You must analyze the person you are going to sell to before interacting with them. Well let's see, when you told me hey excuse me I can ask you a favor, you got my full attention, people like to help another as a matter of course, that was very good.

However you lost me when you flattered me the wrong way. You said hey you are very handsome; would you like to go out with me? You lost me there because your intention was to make a joke, but I felt a bit harassed, in addition to not knowing you and it is rare that someone on the street asks you to go out with you without even knowing you.

Also, you did not analyze me personally, you only said what they taught you at school, because I am a man and I am not attracted to boys, maybe that speech could work for a girl, although maybe I also reject you for the harassment of her person.

Also be careful because your joke speech can be misinterpreted and what we want is not to lose the client and that the speech is brief and concise so that they do not lose their attention on you and we go on sale.

I think if what your intention was to like yourself, for example, you could say... "Hey, how well you look, you can see that you exercise!" or if it was a lady, hey what nice shoes you bring.

That works more with the client, praising something that you see that that person is interested in, more than his body or his face, the activities that he or she carry out are more convenient.

- Ok after you achieve a smile on the client, yes, enter your sales SPEECH, instead of saying something like help me because I can no longer cope with this economy (The client may think well, neither do I, but look at me here I am making you want) Better tell him:

Look here (and you give him the palette), I have these pallets that I am selling, to help me with the expenses of my studies. Can you help me by buying me one or three popsicles? Don't you ever tell him, will you buy me a Popsicle? Because the client will think between yes or no, but instead you say: Can you buy me one or three popsicles? Your mind will quickly think between just those two options:

- Shall I buy you one or three? - Anyway, he or she will already be thinking about buying you.

Now it is very important that you give the product in your hand, we are sensory people, if he or she is already touching the product, and they are already feeling it with their hands, there is a 95% chance that they will buy it from you.

All things have a special vibe, and create desire, you do not have it yet, it is not yours yet, but you can have it, put a price on the item he or she already wants your product.

You already imagined if you are going to eat it, or maybe you fell from the sky because it is what you needed, because that sweet is going to be given to someone special at home or at work, I do not know, but he or she already wants your product. Now if you put a price on it, try to sell the 3 pieces and close the deal: A palette for you, one for your mom and one for your girlfriend.

Ready you already sold, now bless your buyer and ask them if they liked your product, recommend it to others.

The young salesman left very happy and even asked me for advice online. I know that he will apply everything he has learned.

"GIVE THE CUSTOMER THE PRODUCT IN HIS HAND"

This giving the product in your hand is super important, you can tell me wonderful things about your product, thousands of stories, but until I have it in my hand I can fall in love with it. Your physical product is your interaction tool:

USE YOUR INTERACTION TOOL

What is your interaction tool? Is that sample product that you give to your client to help you sell...?

Let the customer know what they can expect from your product.

This is very varied and depends on a lot of what you are selling.

For example, have you seen in malls how there are counters that prepare food with the brand they sell? And they give you a little taste to get to know their product, well that little taste is their interaction tool. You pass your cravings and therefore you try, if you like, right there the lady offers you packages of what she is preparing and sometimes even a gift item when buying two, also (interaction tool) so you can meet other flavors and consume more of their products.

What if it works? Of course it works super, and the big vendors know it ... One day when I was leaving the farm I was very hungry, and passing by a food stand a man gave evidence of little pigs (homemade bread in the shape of a pig) I came to eat the sample and of course I bought.

But the gentleman did not sell one, he sold bags of 5 pieces of little pigs of bread, indeed my craving and my hunger made me buy a complete bag, it served me to eat and even to share.

> "IF YOU DON'T HAVE AN INTERACTION TOOL ... CREATE IT"

The interaction tool is super powerful to sell, remember that I told you that I spent time selling music, well, when I sang a song, I would come to the table and offer my product:

Good evening, like a song for the lady, I said to the client and handed him my Music Menu, which is the list of songs that I know.

(My interaction tool) The man received my musical menu in his hand and to reaffirm the sale even before I chose any song, I would say to him: Thank you, Lord, you are a great gentleman; please dedicate a beautiful song to him.

You see what I did, create a commitment, the man does not even know what song he is going to choose, but the girl next to him is eager and curious to know what song the man who comes with her will dedicate to her.

With emotion it is difficult to choose one, the names of the most romantic songs do not come to your mind, but my menu is a special tool it is divided into themes and artists to make it easier to dedicate a song, there is even a section that is called "Serenades", which has helped many of my clients get out of trouble and dedicate a good song that really makes the lady fall in love.

But what really makes the lady fall in love is that the gentleman next to her dedicates a song to her from the heart and sings it with me. There are already very few gentlemen who dedicate love songs live. Now they are dedicated electronically and remotely, that does not have the same impact as a live song in full color.

I remember that one day I had lost my interaction tool (My Musical Menu) and there were quite a few people in the restaurant but the strange thing is that nobody asked me for songs.

If I sang a song and went on to offer, but people normally at that time do not remember the names of the songs and they did not ask me, I could not sell, because I did not have my interaction tool with me.

For someone who already consumes your product, they already know what to order and they even know the order of the songs they are going to request, but for someone new, who is just getting to know your product, needs something physical to see what you are doing.

Offering.

Yes you can tell him, but it is not the same as feeling it in your hands. The Interaction tool must be physical, and must be able to touch, feel, or taste. In a filthy way it is difficult to create expectations in your client and easier for them to reject your sale.

Literally since I didn't have my tool, I had to create one.

I left the restaurant for a moment, got a small notebook and pen, and began to write down all the songs that I was normally asked for, the best known and that I knew the customer might be interested in.

With that same notebook I returned to my client, he who had already rejected me for not knowing what to ask for, and as if by magic, he hired me, I told him to apologize for the notebook, and that he knew a lot more songs, but that's what I had at the moment. It worked because with that I contract.

The next day I printed the New Menu on my computer, already renewed with the new songs, every week I had homework at least they asked me for one or two new songs, with that my work became very popular because they saw that I did learn the songs that asked me.

Many of my competition fellow musicians, said yes to the client and the songs were not learned.

I have a special rule, if the client asks me for a new song and I commit myself to it, I learn it, yes for the next time you see it I have not learned your song, I will give you 3 more songs. It is already a commitment. Furthermore, that same rule has helped me to become more clients and a broader repertoire.

It has happened to me that I learn the song the following week and the client does not go, but it does not matter because by chance another client asks me for it and, as if I have it, he pays me.

When my old client comes, he is happy, because although time has passed, I did comply and I have the product that he requested. And just for that detail, that client buys me again and even recommends me with other clients.

This sales rule is also applied by the Chinese. If a buyer comes to order a product and they do not have it, they are already looking for a way to get it and have it in their stores.

Your interaction tool is something very important.

It is so simple to do, that it only takes a little of your time to make, but I assure you that if you elaborated your interaction tool you would achieve much more sales.

What you have to add: Only your catalog of products that you sell, with images to make it more attractive to the eye if possible and a phone to place your orders.

If you do not know how to do it here, I will leave you an email so that you can contact us and we will help you prepare it franciscodiemmanuel@gmail.com with pleasure and so that you can maximize your sales.

> **"YOUR TALENT CAN TAKE YOU TO**
>
> **TRAVEL AROUND THE WORLD"**

You do not know how this simple tool has served me, because it gives the client a broader picture of what you are selling, even thanks to that catalog I had many events at home, national and outside the country, private music classes and many friends for the world, all thanks to offering a cell phone and a website where people could learn more about my work.

I was able to go to work in Cancun, Guerrero, Havana, Cuba, Thank God, projects in the United States in Los Cabos, Baja California and Mexico City, among others.

AGREE THE PRICE OF YOUR PRODUCT FROM THE BEGINNING

Agreeing on the price from the beginning of your interaction with the client is of utmost importance and will take the headaches out of you and your client.

Something I really love is sales, because thanks to them, it is that I was able to significantly increase my earnings, much more clearly to be a simple employee.

By working on my own, with my own work team, many times I was able to decide, how much I wanted to earn that week, however, as the saying "the higher the gain, the greater the responsibility" I had to deal with the customer, interaction and negotiation with him and closing deals.

This strengthened me a lot as a seller and allowed me to offer better quality and price to all my clients.

When you sell a physical product itself, any merchandise that comes to your mind, such as clothing, fabrics, food, a drink etc. whatever comes to your mind. The latter has a price already established to go to market, that is to say, for sale. But if your business is entertainment, the price can vary a lot; it all depends on the quality and the place where you offer your product.

I'm going to put it like this, in the restaurant where I work is a 5-star restaurant located in a well-known tourist center in the very center of the country, there are many people who are dedicated to sales, merchants, artisans, street musicians, clowns, dancers and actors.

I am fortunate to be one of the select musicians hired by the company (The downtown restaurant chain).

I can offer my services to the public, inside and outside the two main restaurants in the square.

And since I partially represent the Restaurant Chain, therefore I have to reflect a great image and professionalism, dressed in a fine suit, tie, and my beautiful white guitar...

(La güera, It´s name) and the price of our songs, well it goes according to the level of our clients. However, outside the restaurant, the tables that are outside in the smoking area are exposed to all the street vendors who worthily earn a living selling their products.

This generates a great competition. For example, another group of musicians come and do not charge anything, they just go to ask for cooperation. And this generates, that we must clarify the price of our songs before playing.

Many times in the beginning, when I was still embarrassed or did not know how to tell the price of our songs to the client, at the end of the work done, it gave me a lot of headaches.

Well, our songs have a special price, but if you do not agree or clarify it well from the beginning with the client, many of them took me by surprise, and they wanted to pay me with a cooperation, when not really, their account was much more big. We offer top quality work and I am not saying that it is wrong for other musicians to ask for cooperation, but let's be honest, there are clients who value your work and the effort and time it takes to learn a song, but there are clients who do not, they don't even give you anything, or they give you very little, far below what your work is worth.

> **AGREE THE PRICE OF YOUR PRODUCT FROM THE BEGINNING**

This is great advice for all my friends who dedicate themselves to art, value their work, many times we enjoy doing our work so much, that in reality, we do not put the fair price that it deserves.

If we measured in hours and effort what it takes to make a work of art, many of our works of art would be invaluable, because many of them are unrepeatable. However, in order to make a living from this or market our art, you have to put a price on the public and if you don't know how to sell, surely and as always the client will look for a way to haggle (or renegotiate) the price.

I studied Fine Arts, due to a computer error, I wanted music and I threw myself into the arts. It was my turn to see how they made magnificent paintings, extraordinary sculptures and squandered them, that is, they accepted very little, almost nothing, for their works. This should not be so, you must value your art and if you do not know how to sell, look for a specialized agent like me who can help you promote and give you the fair price that your work deserves. I do not regret having been in that school, I learned many beautiful things.

I remember that one day a client came to me, he was Mexican but he lived in New York (United States of America), he spoke in English, so I negotiated with him in English:

-Hi nice to meet you would you like a song? (Hello, very pleased, would you like a song?) I said, he answered yes and I liked that he asked me for a lot of Mexican music; especially he liked the songs of the immortal Pedro Infante.

Already making friends with him, he confessed what I just told you, that he came to Mexico to buy good Mexican art (crafts and others) for three pesos (meaning very little money) here in Mexico, and sold them in the United States in lots of dollars.

That was his business.

And all because art schools do not teach their students to sell. To sell themselves as artisans and to sell their art for a fair price.

So it is very important that if you are an artist or have a friend or family member who is dedicated to the arts, you give them a copy of this book. So they learn to sell and not see the face of what?

It does not matter if you are a dancer, actor, musician, businessman, teacher, engineer, we must all learn the art of selling.

An engineer himself is already making a new art by creating a new application that helps the world, he uses technology yes, but it is also an art to do things as one can do them. And if you learn the art of selling, I assure you that your work, what you have created, will not stay to consume dust, it can come to light and that the world will see and enjoy it.

It took me a long time to start writing this book, but now it came to light and it can help you and me to have a better life, a dignified life through sales.

Imagine that each of us sold with dignity what we do. This world would be wonderful. Each of the services we paid for would be excellent and they would always receive you with a smile. There would no longer be people disgusted by the bad service because we would all be doing what we are most passionate about and we would be receiving profits for it...

Once upon a time, a very beautiful client answered that she did not love her work, which she wanted to be a great dancer, but she had to dedicate herself to something else to achieve the material goods that she wanted.

Unfortunately like her there are many people, who spend endless hours at a job, who don't like it, which is not their thing, but they do it, because they receive a payment at the end of the month. That is torturing your own being.

If these people learned how to sell, they could even earn a lot more than they earn now and doing what they like.

The first times that I started working on what I like. I could not believe how I had in my hands the profits from doing what I am passionate about. Doing what you like and getting others to pay for it is wonderful. At first I didn't believe it but it is real. It requires work and learning to sell ... Yes.

But it's wonderful that you get paid for what you love.

And there is a saying:

> **"TO NEVER WORK AGAIN ...**
>
> **WORK IN WHAT YOU LIKE"**

I feel great when I get paid to sing a song, a concert or give a conference, for teaching how to sell to others is wonderful. But what gives you the most satisfaction is that people recognize your work. And because you do what you love, you do it very well, every day you prepare more to give 150% of your work. And if they ask more of you or of what you do, you don't get angry for having to work more, on the contrary you do it with a lot of satisfaction and therefore you get better.

If you ask me if I would return to work as I did before enjoying this secret. That I worked more than 12 hours in a job that I did not like, that I hardly saw my family and only because they paid me very well at the end of the month. I would say no, because once you learn to sell, freedom is the gift that comes with selling.

Even working in a company, if you like what you sell, what you represent, you will do your job with all the love and dedication that is required. As they say LITERALLY:

> **"WEAR THE SHIRT"**

Put on the company shirt and learn everything you can, because that will make you level up and profit. There are many companies with which you can make a career. Some even support you with your studies. Get ready and do your best.

And if you work on your own, well, it's time to try harder and keep learning day by day, look for more books like this or follow the link on our website, where we give courses and conferences at home and online:

franciscodiemmanuel@gmail.com

https://francisco-di-emmanuel.negocio.site/

HANDLE PROMOTION PACKAGES

> **"HANDLE PROMOTION PACKAGES"**

If it is printed and in view of the customer, the best, you will save the customer time, looking for what is within their pocket and also save time for you as a seller, because you do not have to be explaining to the customer what the prices are or what products your package contains, he will see it on screen, or in advertising and decide which one is best for his economy.

This trick is well known and handled by fast food business chains. Since service must be prompt, cordial and / or express, the longest time a box seller can save on service is of utmost importance.

It is also for the benefit of the customer as well, since he is already so used to fast food that he wants his food as soon as possible.

You have next to your sales catalog or interaction tool the menu of prices and packages available for the customer to see and can make a quick decision. How does it usually work? Well an example: per piece this product comes out for as much money $$$ but if you choose this package that already includes everything you want and a piece of gift comes out in both ...

So place the packages according to the promotions you manage, for the benefit of the client and your company and show them.

If you work on your own, well you can also:

Once I was shopping in the city center and I was very hungry, I saw a taco stand and I felt like asking for an order.

You already know how rich they are, with their corn tortilla, meat, onion, coriander and sauce to taste.

Well, there were some foreigners who spoke in English and did not know whether to try the tacos; it was their first time in the country.

I went up to them and spoke to them in English, I told them that the tacos in that place were great, that they will try the tacos but be careful with the sauce, not to add too much to your tacos, because it did bite a lot.

Well, when they saw me eat my so happy, they also asked for some tacos, when they finished eating and did the check, the foreigners asked what, how much should they pay? To which the seller did not know how to speak English but was very resourceful.

With the large calculator at her side, she only set out to count. I show the numbers from the calculator to foreigners and voila, they paid in pesos. And the lord gave them their change.

You see this trick is very good, especially when I had clients in my restaurant that had already had a little, when they told them how much they owed us, they always gave me buts and they haggled over the price.

I applied the calculator and it worked, they paid me without reproach and they even gave me a tip. You see how the things we can see with our eyes are recorded better than what we hear with our ears, teach the price in something visual to your customers, it is much better when it comes to selling.

"OFFERS A QUALITY PRODUCT"

Offering a quality product is of utmost importance, there may be a lot of competition, people who may sell the same as you, or similar to you, but the difference lies in the quality of the product that you offer.

Once they asked me - Why do you give a song for $ 100 pesos if the Trio gives 3 songs for the same price...?

- The answer is simple, because the quality is not the same.

I tell you here there are three types of musicians, the good, the bad and the ugly. There are the bad and the ugly... and here are the good ones.
With a single song that you ask me, you will see the difference.

That arouses the interest of the person who listens to you, encourages them to ask you for a song. But be careful, you must give the quality you claim in your speech or the client will not ask you for one more.

Normally when listening to me the client is happy and asks for at least 5 more songs. All our songs are guaranteed, (he said) the one who doesn't like double pay...

It is important to offer a good product, and convince yourself that what you sell is the best. And if not, find a way to make your product the best...

Once I got to the famous basket tacos, I was very hungry and when the man served me, I couldn't help but laugh and I said to him:

- no friend, what is this? I want tacos for men, not for children, look, their tacos are very small, and with this I do not cover a tooth. The man grumbled but said nothing. I advised him that his tacos were too small to make them normal in size and people would like them more.

The man replied that to give them cheaper he had to do it like this.
Imagine if the basket tacos themselves are a bit smaller than the normal tortilla, these were half the half of the tortilla, they were mini-mini tacos.

They looked literally like a small omelets with a smeared bean, they had no taste. I told him that it is useless to give a very cheap product, if people are not going to like it and will never consume it again. Better give them at a higher price, I said, but make a good taco for people to come back. I paid for my tacos and left, I never ate there again.

"STRENGTHEN AND DO A BETTER JOB"

Every effort has its rewards. When I just started to put together the repertoire that I wanted to offer to my clients, it was difficult, I didn't know where to start, but once I started and gave structure to my work, everything was easier.

Just tell me to gather the information and empty the information.

I have friends and classmates who took the TEACHERS (Diploma for English Teachers) with me and could not be certified, because they have not been able or have not known how to start their Thesis (Written research work that they require to obtain the academic degree).

And I know, I went there, but the important thing is to sit at the computer and start, if you never start you will never finish it. I remember that when I started the thesis it happened to me like 2 literal hours, just thinking about how it was going to be, I looked for examples on the internet to give me an idea...

And boom! I started writing, formatting, structuring, and even planning on a piece of paper. In the end it was worth it, you can deliver a great job.

And what I say is true, my friends and colleagues had planned to certify together, but at the end of all of us, only two achieved the academic title, a colleague and me. Today some years have passed and I ask my friends that if they were able to deliver their thesis and they say no, they have left it for peace.

All because they haven't even started trying to do it. Hey! every day, a little bit, if it doesn't work, we will try again, until it works.

In the end, I thought that what they left out is a good business proposal for you and me, but if they know how to do their thesis, I could help them by advising them and at the same time earn good money.

My friends win and I Win (It's a Win-Win).

> **INVEST IN NEW KNOWLEDGE**
>
> ...
>
> **THAT WILL ALWAYS BRING YOU BETTER PROFITS "**

Offering a job or product of literal quality becomes easier over time, you just have to try harder and listen to what your client's needs are.

Think, if you were the customer, would you buy your own product? And if not, what would you do to improve it? Write down all the recommendations your client tells you, as you are the seller, you are in love with your product, but the client, who is your main consumer, can add to your product the cherry on the cake, which will make it even better.

I believed that with the wide repertoire that I have, I would no longer have homework, but every week I have at least one or two new songs that my client asks me to learn.

It is like a doctor, new diseases come out and the doctor must know with what new medicine to attack them.

The same is here you must renew every certain time to improve your product or update it with the new needs that the client requires.

I never thought to get to the point of needing a special terminal to be able to charge my new customers with a card.
But it was the same customer who one day told me to buy my terminal and I would have much more income.
I remember that once we were hired by a man who came from Paris, he liked our work a lot and hired us by the hour.

At the end of the day, his account was so large that he was unable to pay us in effect and our client was half toned with the alcohol he drank, we had to accompany him to the ATM about three times, because he was taking out more money and wanted more music, I made more money and asked for more songs.

So we stayed until about 3 in the morning. If he had had my terminal at that time, we could have charged him right there, without having to get up from his place in the restaurant.

"GET YOUR TERMINAL TO CHARGE EASIER"

On another occasion we had a couple of boyfriends visit us in the restaurant.

They were very excited asking for songs, so much so that even the next table was also excited, with the live music.

As the two couples were living together and singing very happily together, I suggested that they join their tables.

They said yes. In the end it was a wonderful and very tiring show, as we were there for several hours. We sang with a lot of energy, but it was worth it in the end the client was happy.

What was the surprise for the group that at the end of the show the account was also high and the young people did not have that amount in cash. They wanted to pay by card, but we had no way to charge them more than in cash.

So again we had to accompany them to the cashier. What was our surprise, which the closest ATM had no money and they needed an ATM from a different bank.

We wasted about an hour looking for an ATM where they could withdraw money and in fear that they might not pay us. There I learned that I definitely had to invest in a terminal, to be able to collect with all the cards, rest for the client, peace of mind also for me.

"ACCEPT THE DIFFERENT FORMS OF PAYMENT"

Accepting other forms of payment will bring you much more profit, I tell you from experience. We have national clients, but I think we have much more foreign clients, who do not actually carry cash, for their safety, and prefer to pay for everything with the card.

If you are hesitating between buying your terminal or not, I advise you to buy it, you will have much more sales and you will be able to give that ease to your client, to be able to pay with another form of payment other than cash and thus you will not let sales go for not updating you.

This world advances more and more towards technology and if you do not take the leap, you will be left behind. I have a friend of mine who is dedicated to the same thing as me, he is older and for the same reason he does not want to update himself, he clings to staying in the 80s and no more does not want to take the leap.

This has caused him to lose many sales, literally the customer does not have to pay him more than in cash and he is not comfortable having to leave his table, his food has cooled and he has to waste time at the ATM to withdraw money and pay my friend. I respect his age and his beliefs, but in this new world it is to renew or die.
Once upon a time on a Sunday morning the phone rang very early.

Sundays are usually my only day that I can usually get up later, the other days I have them full of activities and my get up is earlier, to start my day with energy.

So that day the phone rang early, it was my friend Enrique who at that time urgently needed my help. Enrique sells fine fabrics in the main square and had convinced a client to make a strong purchase, but he could not charge her because he did not have a terminal and the client could only pay by card. I remember that I was very excited the day I bought my terminal, which of course I went and told all the benefits I had to my friend Enrique.

Well today was the day he urgently needed my help. He asked me if I could run to the plaza at that moment and take my terminal, or the sale would get out of hand. I said yes, to give me 5 minutes to get dressed, pour water and run to the plaza where he was.

The good thing is that the day before I had gone to visit my parents and I had stayed there to sleep, how lucky for my friend that my parents' house is very close to Enrique's work and that day I had stayed there to sleep. . I got dressed and ran to the plaza in search of my friend; I was wearing my tailor suit from work that day.

When my friend Enrique and his mother arrived, they were super happy, the client was still there. I took out my terminal and I charged her client, my friend did better that day because instead of selling a single piece, as the client saw that if she could charge the card herself, she preferred to take three more pieces.

In other words, their sales rose much more just because they could charge with the card. And even more so, the friend who came with the client, feeling safe when it came to collecting merchandise, did not fall behind either, so she also bought four other pieces for her, with her respective credit card.

In the end I only dedicated myself to closing the sale with the collection and the sending of your digital voucher (proof of purchase) to the customer's private phone. You see my friend not only did not lose the sale that day, he was able to sell not only one piece but 8 pieces in that same instant.

Can you imagine the smile of my selling friend Enrique and his mom? When I told them that I could get them a terminal for them, they did not hesitate to collect the money and asked me to bring them their terminal, because when they saw everything they have sold with their new terminal, it ended up paying for itself. In the end they discovered that it was a great investment.

DIVERSIFY YOUR PRODUCTS YOU WILL EARN MUCH MORE

When we have a star product, the one with which we are earning a lot of money, we think that the work has already stopped there.

And it is not like that, people are left with more desire to consume another class of your products.

And you have to diversify for them, which are the key of the business, to have several sources of income, not only from your star product, but also from similar products that the client could buy together with your star product.

For example, when people go to the circus to enjoy a great juggling and clown show, it doesn't stop there, paying only for a ticket to see the show, no. People get hungry and thirsty, you can sell them popcorn, sweets, hot dogs, soft drinks etc.

In addition, children usually go to the functions, well sell them colorful lights, sweets, toys, everything you can think of that your client would like to consume. Many vendors forget about this and it is of utmost importance:

When you sell a toy to a child and take it home, his cousins go and this boy shows off his toy, which you think his cousins want to make, they will not say to their parents:

- Dad, take me to the circus because the show is very nice - No... They are going to go with their parents and they are going to demand that they take them to the circus, because they want a toy just like the one that their cousin has!!! . Do you see how this toy is a great marketing stimulus, ideal to enhance your sales? (You must diversify).

There was a pretty lady who used to stand outside the cinema and sell some stuffed animals, so pretty, that she herself had made (hand-knitted). How did she know when the movie premieres were? I don't know, I guess he was doing his research. The joke is that when we were children, all my friends and I wanted to buy her, they were toys that you couldn't find anywhere else.

You want to diversify, it is very easy, you are a musician and you sing very well... record an album and sell it at the end of your presentations, people will recommend you and may even know you more about your album.

You are a dancer or dancer, record yourself and sell your choreography for XV years and Weddings. This last of the weddings is a Boom Right now and is booming. You are a seller, open your website and sell everything you can online and at home.
Open a YouTube channel so that people know your talents.

I know a businessman friend that his company sells building materials. Well, he applied my knowledge and now he has a YouTube channel where he records his best workers doing remodeling work and at the same time announces the products that my businessman friend sells in his company.

Now he sells not only here but throughout the world and has opened a transport distribution chain to be able to take his product to the United States and all of Latin America.

"UPLOAD YOUR TALENT TO DIGITAL PLATFORMS"

Recording you and uploading your videos to the network has served me wonderfully, many times at the time of negotiations people still do not fully know your work and need to see and know about you, as I do, uploading videos to my own page of content, where not only people can enjoy my work but they also see the positive comments that good people who know my work put on my channel.

From this I have another specialized book that if you want you can buy "HOW TO SELL ONLINE - BY FRANCISCO DI EMMANUEL" in which I teach you step by step dedicated mind of what you must do to maximize your profits selling online.

It is fully guaranteed and you can get it at the following link:

franciscodiemmanuel@gmail.com

I highly recommend it and don't forget, always investing in yourself and your knowledge will generate much more profit.

"INVEST IN YOU AND YOUR KNOWLEDGE"

LISTEN TO CUSTOMER NEEDS

Always listen to your client's needs and find how to solve them, write them down in a special notebook, or somewhere, because they may be lost. And these suggestions will always be well rewarded by your client.

I remember once an elderly man asked me for a special song. It was a very old song, but he liked to sing it to his wife.

The first time I met them, he and his wife came together and they almost didn't hire me, all because they didn't know that song.

The man asked me to sing other beautiful songs to his wife: boleros, ballads, rancheras, but none of them satisfied exactly what his wife wanted to hear. I guess it was a special melody between them.

The man paid me for the few songs he sings and I promised that when I saw them again, I would already have the special song that his wife asked me for.

Time passed and there were many coincidences that happened later. It turns out that his wife's favorite song was from a very good, but now deceased composer named Gonzalo Curiel.

And in the time that passed after I saw the lord and his wife. A very pretty and elegant girl had come to work as a receptionist at the restaurant. I do not normally talk much with the ladies who receive people, to avoid misunderstandings with colleagues and the company.

But I saw that I paid great attention to this, especially when I sang good boleros. Well, as if not making friends with this young lady, it turned out that she was the granddaughter (so to speak) of the composer Gonzalo Curiel himself. How small the world is and how great the coincidences are.

This aroused much more interest in me to learn the new song that the man and his wife asked me for. And when I finally saw them again I was ready. The gentleman did not want to hire me, but when he heard that I already knew his wife's favorite song, he not only hired me but I spent all afternoon singing for them, he paid me and even tipped me for my good effort.

Since I am financially free, time no longer passes for me. I even ran into a few clients that have been 3 years since I last sang for them. I was glad to know that they remembered me; in fact they still brought a video where they recorded me singing with them. And believe it or not, they did ask me for their songs.

You could forget about the customer's face. But the client will never forget you, because he not only remembers you, but the experience he lived with you.

LEAVE YOUR CLIENT HAPPY AND SCHEDULE IT FOR A FUTURE SALE

It is important that the client remains happy, comfortable with what you do, but above all wanting more of your work.

Many times I was touched by clients who did not bring much money to enjoy my product, especially young people, but although they could only hire me a song, I gave them an extra one.

And I told them not to worry when they come back I know that you will hire me many more songs (this is to look good and schedule your client for an upcoming visit) People were happy to receive an extra song for free.

It did not take more than 5 minutes more of my time, but my clients were grateful, and very satisfied, and I promise you that more than one if you returned to me.

And they said to me –Do you remember that when I came with my girlfriend or so-and-so, you sang to us and gave us a song and we promised to return? Well, here we are. - People do remember what you do for them and know how to reward you.

I did not sell merchandise at that time, nor songs or music, I sold incredible and unrepeatable moments that they shared with their families and loved ones. And they always, always remember me.

There was even a girl who came with her friends and asked me for a song, she interrupted me in the middle of the show and secretly told me, sorry, I don't have money to pay you, my friends are inviting me.

I said don't worry about this song that is from the house. When you come back again you will hire me many times.

My surprise was that all her friends cooperated to pay me for that song, although I had already told them it was from the house, and even so the girl recommended me to her parents and on the day of their anniversary I took them to the restaurant and they hired me for their celebration.

You see, always leave a good impression with your clients and they will return to you.

If you sell merchandise and think that you cannot apply this form of sale, give them a happy moment: a joke, a good comment, a God Bless you and very important, give them a phone number where they can call you to hire you.

> **"THE NUMBER IS MORE IMPORTANT THAN THE CARD"**

Some may disagree on this issue, but let me tell you, it really works.

To me it is very professional of you that you have physical cards, where you're data, address and your phone come, where the client can locate you.

But from experience I tell you that we saw that now, at present it was a useless expense, because we distributed thousands of cards and very few spoke to us, also sadly we saw that we found them forgotten at the table or on the floor, and the client when he was looking for I never found your calling card because I had forgotten it at the restaurant.

"APPLY THE DIGITAL CARD"

To solve this, we applied a better strategy, we made a new tool, a "Digital Card" (An image of a card with all our data but digital)

And every time we made a sale, we asked the customer for their WhatsApp number to send them your voucher and our new "Digital Card" as well as some extra promotions such as Video Call Serenades, Live Events, Online and Home Classes etc.

We also used to add their number to our client portfolio. And the client would never lose us again because he also had us registered on his phone.

"NEVER REFUSE A GOOD CUSTOMER"

There was a client that I liked very much, he hired us two or three times, and he always said that he wanted to take us to work in Paris France, he said that Mexican music was highly appreciated there and that we would earn many Euros. I keep waiting for the man who was going to take us to Paris.

One fine day we were already working at a special table in the restaurant and a Cuban family made up of three people arrived, Dad, Mom and their 14-year-old daughter, they wanted us to attend them and sing some songs for them, since They were leaving and they wanted to listen to us, before leaving, but we were already attending to another table.

The insistence of the lord of Cuba was so great and I do not like to look bad on anyone, that we asked the table where we were to please to give us permission to sing three songs to the family that was requesting us.

We did so and they were very happy with their three songs. We come back with our client first and all good, everyone happy.

Sometime later it was a Sunday day and there was not much work in the restaurant. I saw a couple in the background bringing a child and I applied myself singing a children's song (you know, when you have a detail with the children, usually the parents have a detail with you) I was in the middle of the song.

When suddenly, after many days had passed, the Cuban Family arrived, if the same one from that time when we could only sing three songs to them, they came to save the day.

I fell like angels from heaven because that day the child's family gave me nothing.

So I offered my service to the incoming family, the Cuban family and what was so beautiful my surprise, that that same day was the birthday of the mother, the wife of the Lord of Cuba and their 14-year-old daughter.

My songs have a high price, but that day the man said to me: - No, no, no, but how much do you charge me boy for 10 songs for my wife? I lowered the price a little and sang him a package of 10 songs and still thank you I gave him some of the house.

They were super happy, so much so that the Lord told me with each song he liked:
- You are earning "YOUR TICKET TO CUBA CHICO!"
- At the end I gave him some of the house, and I was surprised, because well, since they were from Cuba, I gave them singing the Guantanamera verses, the song, I tell them that I was surprised because in the middle of the melody the Lady was he stopped singing with me.

He answered me with other very nice verses from his beloved Cuba... "I cultivate a white rose in June as in January... I cultivate a white rose for the sincere friend ... Who gives me his frank hand. And before I die I want to take my verses from the soul: Guantanamera Guajira Guantanamera" (Cuban poet and political writer José Marti). In that the applause was immediate and the Lady's husband, very happy, told me:

- YOU WON YOUR TICKET TO CUBA!!!

- I left him my details and he promised to call me.

> "YOUR WORK CAN TAKE YOU TO TRAVEL AROUND THE WORLD"

The man was very excited that he went with them, to his beloved Cuba to sing with his daughter who would be fifteen. Its fifteen springs and he wanted us to sing live, in front of his family and all his guests.

I must be honest, for a moment I did not know if they were actually going to speak to me or leave us standing like the supposed gentleman who would take us to France did.

I faithfully gave him my details and waited for him to speak to me.

What was my surprise that a month later my phone rang: - Well, who's talking? - Good afternoon, the Lord of Cuba speaks. Could we meet this Sunday at my house so that we can agree on your trip to Cuba, please? - Of course I did, I answered see you there.

I had to go to his house to find out if the trip to Cuba was actually going to be and prepare myself, and also because the man said to me: "Yes, I have to introduce my mother and my people, because nobody is going to Cuba with me if you don't know my people before.

That day I arrived at his house and they very kindly prepared to eat me, a delicious Cuban food.

But before I had to speak to the Lord of Cuba and be very sincere: (they know that, above all, a seller must be sincere with his client for a good agreement)

- Excuse me, what is your name? - Leo - He answered me... I am very worried Leo, because you tell me that you are taking me and any of my group or family that I want to take, and the truth is that I would not want to keep the commitment and that at the very least don't do it. I told him what the Lord of France told us, that he took us and he took us and at the mere hour he never took us.

I told him look Leo what you think: (sincerity above all) I still do not have my passport to leave the country. I charge $$$$$$$ both here in Mexico for such an event.

If you gave me half the event in advance, with that money I assure you that you are going to take me, because you already gave me half the event and you would assure me that I will go, because I would already have my papers in order (my passport and others) and I could go with you and your family.
Not only that, we agreed that he would pay me every weekend for the rehearsals he had with his daughter and my visa to be able to travel.

My experience in Cuba was wonderful, the friends from there treated me like one of the family, they took me to know Old Havana, New Havana, the boardwalk, "The House of Music" The Museum of Che Guevara, The hotel Main of Cuba and many tourist places.

They used to ride me in a 1957 luxury car, the kind that only appears in movies. Our event went very well; we were congratulated a lot for our performance, especially Yssell my student.

Yssell almost made me cry when he dedicated one of his XV years candles to me and just before our show, I had to hold back my tears of emotion in order to put on a good show. In the end everything went very well.

They took me to serenade over there the family and friends of my friend Leo and they always gave me delicious food, traditional Cuban food. They treated me like King, like a great friend.

I have a lot to tell, but if you are interested I will tell you about it in another book because they are very interesting and interesting things that I experienced there. Especially:

> "TRAVEL
>
> YOU CAN CHANGE YOUR
>
> OVERVIEW OF THE WORLD
>
> "

I want to dedicate this part of the book to thank with all my heart, now to my friends in Cuba: Leo, his Wife Mayrelis, his daughter Yssell and now my student and all his family from La Bellísima Habana Cuba who treated me excellent, as to one more son...

Above all, Mama Juana from Cuba, her children, Leo's sister-in-law who cooks so richly, her brother Leo who took us everywhere in those 1957 luxury cars with a Toyota engine, or the Mexican friend "Mi Banda me endorse "

Betsy, the young people I met there, who dance well, and the girls when they get ready look like models, Morelos's sister and her husband who inspired part of this book with their anecdotes, my fellow friends, the teachers of music, to all Leo's friends who invited me a drink where they saw me:

- Mexican, Mexican! Have this Roncito or this little wine...

Hehehe - To the Cuban embassy that I treat myself so respectfully, in short, everyone, and everyone.

There was something I experienced there that had a great impact on me and inspired this book to come out much sooner. And is that the world is so small, that many of the economic problems we suffer here also suffer in other countries.

Being at the XV party, I remember very well that the Husband of Mayrelis's sister, that is, her brother-in-law of Mayrelis confessed to me:

- Professor the world here is not so different than there, where you live, I am a chemical engineer and I work in the best company in the country making yogurt to sell in the big stores.

That yogurt that you see in the supermarket that is sold on the stock market, we do it, however I receive a salary for it and even so with my salary and that of my wife who is a nurse it is not enough for me to live better.

- Two salaries, of two great professionals and barely enough for what is necessary. And it is that Leo my friend from Cuba explains to me that there in Havana they have another monetary regime.

He tells me that here in Mexico he earns in thousands and there in Cuba in pennies, that is to say that although the two parents are professionals, they can never aspire to earn a higher salary.

That story really touched my soul and here in my country we do not have that regime, however the wages of a normal worker are also very low. But if we only learned here in my country how to sell correctly, maybe things would change.

I love to share that since I learned to sell my life changed for good and forever. I worked many things in my youth, I was a blacksmith, carpenter, musician, dancer, packer, and I worked in large companies as a salesman, cashier, floor manager and Head of Department.

I worked in security; I was a military man, commander and teacher. And he charged very well for it, but nothing raised my profits, and he potentiated my cash flow (cash flow) so much until I learned to sell, found a company, market a product, etc. etc.

Now I am free work at my own pace, I finished my degree, and I continue studying another, I see my family more time and I like what I do and I enjoy when my client also enjoys my work and even recommends me.

Learn to Sell is the Best Investment you can make for your whole life.

LEARN TO SELL ONLINE

We are in the new world and not only do you have to learn to sell; you have to learn to market your product all over the world. Remember, I don't win very well because I only bought one client. I earn very well, because thousands of clients come to me to consume my product.

"THE SECRET

IT IS TO HAVE SEVERAL

SOURCES OF INCOME"

Not only have a customer, but have many interested customers who want to buy from you.

For this you must generate trust, remember if you are not in the network, you simply do not exist and the consumer now is very capricious, he wants to know about you before consuming your product.

I remember once my old cell phone had already broken down.

You must know a little secret about me, that my phone is no longer just my entertainment or to make calls, no, my phone has now become my main tool for my work, it is my personal computer and on the go, all the information I need to send my clients videos, catalogs, menus of the items I have for sale, promotions and even information so that they can make deposits from anywhere in the world.

I manage my sales channel, my YouTube channel and my website from my cell phone.
So my Smartphone has become, without being offended by my secretary, my ideal personal assistant.

For the same reason I need a phone of a higher range, which has all the necessary functions so that I can do my work over the network.

I remember I raised a little money, well actually enough money I would say, and I went to the shopping plaza to find the phone I needed.

When I got there the young lady took great care of me. He offered me the phones he had on display and there were two in particular that caught my attention.

One of a brand already recognized with everything I needed and at the price I had in my portfolio.

And another one that was from a not so well-known brand but that "brought everything I wanted" (in quotes) but also some super video games and great virtual reality glasses.

That they were used only for that device.

I must confess that as a child I was born in the new era, I am a fan, a fan of video games, if I know I am already an adult with a family, but sorry that is my delusion, I am a lover of new technologies.

Well the decision was difficult, both cost exactly the same, but ... I did not know the phone of that different brand and that to me, gave me a little mistrust.

The young lady I think she despaired of seeing me compare the two phones, turning them up and down, but she could not see them on because they did not have enough battery (error of the seller because if she wanted to make a sale, I would have put both phones to charge).

Finally, indecisive because I didn't know which one I wanted to take, the store closed me and I couldn't buy anything. When you get home, do you know what was the first thing I did when I got home? I started researching the products of both brands online. And that's where I was able to make my decision:

The unbranded phone that I was so insistent that the lady buy, was very nice on the outside, it even attracted the buyer with its video games and virtual glasses, but all that did not compensate for the processor it brought.

I started to read a lot of negative comments from people who had bought the same phone and it didn't work for them, to top it off the company was Indian and there wasn't an agency here in the country where they could make their guarantee. The seller wanted to make her sale but was not honest with her product or omitted important details that I should know before purchasing or not her product. The answer was obvious, thanks to my research I opted for the best phone that was from the well-known brand and so I did not risk my capital foolishly, but went to the safe.

"LEARN TO SELL ONLINE"

If you want to know how you can learn online I ask you to look for my new book "LEARN TO SELL INTERNET BY FRANCISCO DI EMMANUEL" play the following link so that you can make your order online:

franciscodiemmanuel@gmail.com

To the Whatsapp phone: 044 55 23 27 74 40

MY WEB PAGE:

https://francisco-di-emmanuel.negocio.site/

There I will teach you:
How to create your own Interaction Menu
How to create your own website for your sales
How to sell through social networks
How to open your YouTube channel and upload your content
How to make your Digital Business Cards

How to sell more online and much more content.

As we know you are already dying to go sell there they go:

THE 10 POINTS OF "THE ART OF SELLING"

BELIEVE IN YOURSELF

Point # 1 believes in yourself and your product...

First of all you have to have confidence in yourself to be able to sell. Believe in yourself and your product. Know that you are special, and you can learn to sell if you set your mind to it.

Every day get up optimistically and aim to learn how to sell.

Write down all your experiences when selling, what served you and what did not serve you also when approaching a client. See what phrases if they worked for you and what attitudes you can change to make your sale more attractive.

To think that what you are selling is going to change the world and it is going to generate profits at the same time.

DRESS WELL

Point number # 2 Dresses very well and according to what you sell...

Dressing well improves your self-esteem, but dressing well according to what you sell improves your sales...

Remember that you are a sales artist, you must go out into the world with your best smile and your best wardrobe, those clothes that represent what you sell... your gala suit, your tuxedo, your hanger uniform, your best dress, polished shoes, successful and successful hairstyle.

Because the world, before hearing what you sell, will first see you from top to bottom, and they will see you as a winner and they will want to know about you and what you are selling. And they will be eager to know what you have to offer. Go out, sell and eat the world in bites.

DO NOT BE AFRAID TO SELL

Point numbers #3 don't be afraid to sell...

To sell is to have in your hands a very precious good or service that you want to offer to others and make an exchange either for money or for another good.

Don't be shy about improving the world with your product.

And yes what it costs you is to talk to others, practice, practice all the time. Sell to them, sell to your friends, sell to your relatives, sell to strangers, that are the basic test, sell to your neighbors, sell to everyone. But sell, practice makes perfect.

Practice your sales speeches (your SPEECH), but more than anything practice socializing with people, talk to them they don't bite, and listen to what they have to say, that's the key to success.

A man and a woman become rich by solving the problems of others and monetizing these events.

KNOW YOUR PRODUCT

Point number # 4 Know your product...

Know your product 100%, its qualities, its defects and its virtues. Knowing what your product does and does not do will help you sell it more easily. Remember, a good knowledgeable customer does not buy anything, but rather knows the product well.

BUILD TRUST

Point number #5 Build trust - Be honest with yourself and with people...

We must create a bond with the client and for that we must be sincere with our words, offer the best we have but always with a smile and with the truth on our lips...

There is no use making the best sale of your life if it will be based on lies, because in the end, the truth always comes out, and it is very certain that your product will be returned to you when the client sees that what you told him about it was not true that product and this will cause you to have losses, losses in sales, losses in products and especially losses in customers.

Do not lose the trust of the client, this is invaluable.

If you are an honest seller and sell your customer what he really needs, do not fear, he will return to you, and will recommend you to others, even some will reward you for your honesty.

CREATE YOUR INTERACTION TOOL

Point number #6 Create your catalog or customer interaction tool...

Remember the customer does not know everything you sell and needs to feel the product in his hands to fall in love with him (from the view of the product love is born) We are sensory people, at the moment of making the sales speech, give him the product you sell in hand, if you accept it you are 95% more likely than if you bought it.

DELIVER A QUALITY PRODUCT

Point number #7 Deliver a quality product...

What differentiates you the most from your competition is your high service and delivering a great quality product?

Quality beats quantity and therefore generates higher profits.

But ask the Manzanita Company if I'm not right.

LISTEN TO YOUR CUSTOMERS

Point number #8 Listen to the needs of your customers...

Listening, writing down and solving the needs that your clients request will bring you more benefits in the short, medium and long term. You will have confident clients who believe in you and have the confidence to recommend your product.

CREATE NEW PACKAGES

AND

PROMOTIONS

Point number #9 Create attractive promotions and packages...

Preferably they are printed so that the client can decide which package or promotion is the most convenient for his pocket.

LEAVE YOUR CLIENT HAPPY

Point number #10 Leave your client happy and wanting to continue consuming your product...

Create pleasant sales experiences, so that the customer not only consumes your product once, but his experience with you and your product is so pleasant that he returns much more to you.

POINT NUMBER 11 AND 12 GIFT:

YOUR DIGITAL BUSINESS CARD

Point number #11 Create your Digital Business card...

Do not lose customers because they can no longer find your number to dial you, ask them for their WhatsApp number and send them your virtual card and promotions.

DIVERSIFY AND SELL ALSO ON THE INTERNET

Point number #12 diversifies your products and also sells online...

Always handle more products that accompany your star product and...

Also learn to sell on the Internet and Social Networks.

Thank you for reading this book, I hope that the content and experiences acquired here can serve to inspire you to be a great seller, that in the company you work you can be part of the team, we really want you to wear your shirt and if You are going to undertake the journey of selling on your own or creating your own company, which is a quality product.

I wish for you to find the financial freedom that you deserve and I ask that you always invest in yourself, in the search for new knowledge. And use them to inspire others to make this world a better world.

Because as I mentioned in this book, if we all learned the art of selling what we love to do the most. We would all be happy in our jobs and as you do what you enjoy, well; work becomes a blessing for you and your clients.

I wish you all the best…

Your friend and Personal Trainer in sales:

FRANCISCO DI EMMANUEL

www.ingramcontent.com/pod-product-compliance
Lightning Source LLC
Chambersburg PA
CBHW071358210526
45465CB00001B/157